Write
Your Own
Story
Book

Write Your Own Story Book

Featuring fabulous stories written by: - - - - - - - - - - - - - - -

- -

If found, please return to: - - - - - - - - - - - - - - - - - - -

- -

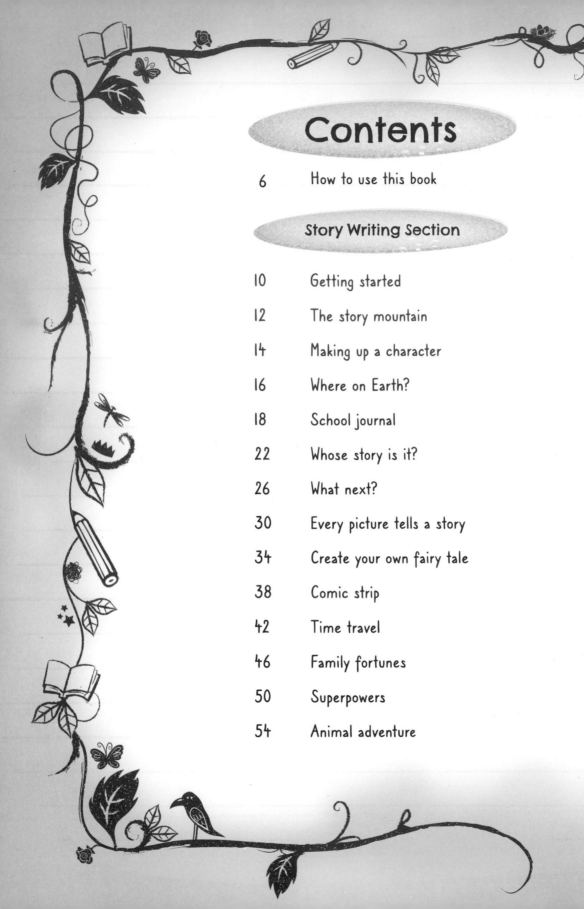

Contents

Story Writing Toolkit

How to use this book

In this book you'll find lots of space to write your own stories, as well as ideas and suggestions to help you become an amazing author. You can start writing right away, or you could turn to the Story Writing Toolkit on pages 82–95 to find some help, with general writing tips and checklists.

There's space for you to write a title for your story here.

Some pages have writing tips to help you.

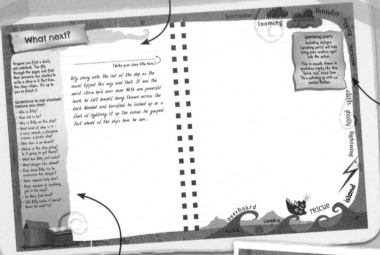

There are story suggestions here, and questions to ask yourself as you're planning what to write about.

Some pages have lists of interesting words that might be useful.

Things you might need:

Pencils

An eraser

Pens

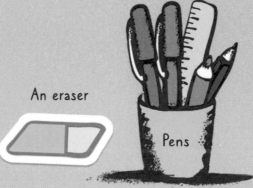

A dictionary

(and maybe a thesaurus)

Your brain

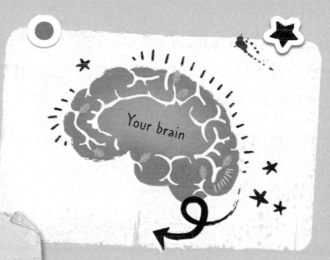

Spare paper to scribble
ideas and plan your
stories on, and to finish
any stories that are too
long to fit in the book

And
some ideas

Story
Writing
Section

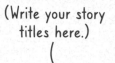

(Write your story titles here.)

Stories contents page

Getting started

(Write your story title here.)

To get you started on your first story, here's an outline with blanks for you to fill in the details.

You could choose characters, settings and actions from the lists on these pages or invent some of your own.

Character suggestions

- clown
- astronaut
- schoolchild
- supervillain
- fairy
- naughty twins
- baby elephant
- explorer
- knight
- talking cat
- detective
- bad-tempered giant
- lonely orphan
- dancer
- sports star
- opera singer
- friendly dinosaur
- cunning sleuth
- long-distance runner
- puppet master

Hello

Once upon a time there was a...
(Describe your main character here.)

Who lived in/went to...
(Describe your setting here.)

One day...
(Something happens to get the story started.)

And so...
(What does your character do next and what does he or she hope might happen as a result?)

However...
(Something goes wrong.)

Then...
(How does your character try to solve the problem?)

Eventually...
(Does your character succeed?)

In the end...
(Bring your story to a close here.)

Setting suggestions

- spooky castle
- deep, dark forest
- long ago
- desert island
- sports stadium
- future city
- king's palace
- little cottage
- boarding school
- beach resort
- mysterious ruins
- underground maze
- land made of cake
- pirate ship
- museum

Possible story starters – the character...

- sets out on a journey
- finds a treasure map
- discovers he or she can fly
- puts on a show
- goes shopping
- enters a contest
- arrives in a strange land
- receives an invitation
- moves house
- decides to have a party
- discovers a secret door
- runs away from home
- becomes invisible
- makes a new friend
- finds a magic pencil

The story mountain

All stories need a beginning, a middle and an end.

Before you start writing a story, it's a good idea to plan an outline of what's going to happen in each part.

One way to do this is to think of your story as a mountain, like this:

Problem
Something goes wrong – a mystery, a dramatic event or a disagreement.

Build-up
Something happens to your characters to start the action.

Resolution
The problem is resolved.

Beginning
Introduce your characters and the setting.

End
The threads of the story are tied up.

Now write an outline for a short story.

Beginning

Build-up

Problem

Resolution

End

Follow your outline to write up your story on this page.

(Write your story title here.)

....

Ups and downs

When you come to plan the outline for a longer story, you might want your character to face more than one problem. So your story mountain may have several peaks.

Making up a character

When you write a story, it's your job to create interesting, believable characters who will capture the reader's imagination.

You don't have to tell the reader everything about your characters, but the more you know about them the more convincing they'll be.

To start building up a character, fill in this diagram with words describing him or her.

Who or what is he, she or it?

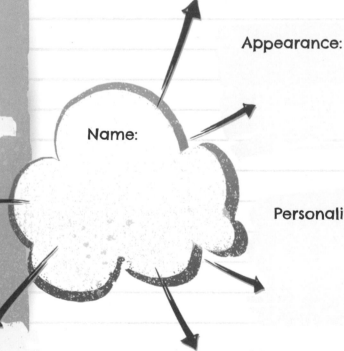

Appearance:

Name:

Strengths and weaknesses:

Personality:

Likes and dislikes:

Goals and ambitions:

A day in the life

Once you've decided what your character is like, it's what he or she says and does in different situations that helps to drive a story. Imagine it's the strangest, most wonderful day of your character's life and write a short story about it.

(Write your story title here.)

....

Acting it out

The best way to bring your character to life is to describe how he or she acts. For example, you don't need to say a character is generous if you show him doing or saying something generous.

You can find more help with building characters on page 86.

Where on Earth?

Whether you set your story in the real world, or a fantasy kingdom, on board a pirate ship or in a toy store, you can make it more vivid by describing the setting in detail.

To help you flex your descriptive muscles, write a letter describing your home to someone who is coming to stay for the first time.

Imagine your guest comes from a foreign land – maybe even another world.

It may all be familiar to you, but what would it look, sound, feel and smell like to a stranger?

Do you have any unusual objects or customs at home that might need to be explained to an outsider?

Dear ....

school journal

One way to get inside the head of a character is to write as though he or she is telling a story about him— or herself, perhaps in a letter or a diary.

This means that — instead of writing about the character as "he" or "she" — you write from the "I" point of view.

Fill in this journal to tell the story of a character's first week at a new school.

Questions to think about

- What kind of school is it?
- What are the teachers like?
- Where is it?
- What classes does it have?
- How is it different from your character's previous school?
- Does he or she join any clubs?
- Who does your character think he or she will be friends with?
- Is there anyone he or she doesn't like?
- Does he or she get into trouble?
- Is there anything next week that your character is looking forward to, or dreading?

Monday :

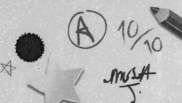

Tuesday:

Wednesday:

playing fields
best friend

library
nervous
uniform
worst enemy
late for class

cheating
teacher's pet
homework
class clown
dormitory

clever
bunsen burners
detention

A-grade
pushing shoving
locker room

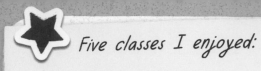

Five classes I enjoyed:

Thursday:

Friday:

The weekend:

My new best friends are:

Whose story is it?

(Write your story title here.

....

1. A story can turn out very differently depending on which character you choose to focus on.

2. Usually, *Cinderella* is told from her point of view. But what if someone else took the spotlight? Try retelling the story from the point of view of one of these characters instead:

The Fairy Godmother

The Wicked Stepmother

Prince Charming

One of the Ugly Sisters

Questions to consider

- What do the other characters think of Cinderella?

- Did the original story get it right? Is the stepmother really wicked? How charming is Prince Charming? Is the Fairy Godmother really kind?

- How does your character feel at the end of the story?

1. Cinderella lives with her father, her stepmother and her two ugly stepsisters.

2. She does all the housework.

3. The stepsisters go off to a ball, but Cinderella has nothing to wear and stays at home.

4. Luckily, she has a Fairy Godmother who conjures up a ball dress and a coach out of rags and a pumpkin.

5. Cinderella CAN go to the ball - but only until midnight, when her finery will turn back into rags.

6. At the ball, Cinderella dances with Prince Charming and they fall in love.

7. Midnight strikes. Cinderella runs away, but loses a shoe.

8. Prince Charming picks up the shoe. He swears to marry the girl whose foot it fits, and searches the kingdom for her.

9. The ugly sisters try on the shoe. It doesn't fit them but it does fit Cinderella.

10. Cinderella marries the prince and they live happily ever after — or do they?

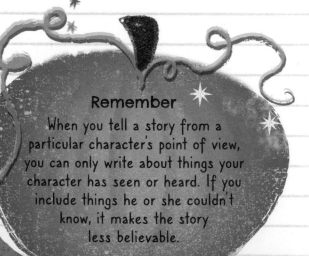

Remember

When you tell a story from a particular character's point of view, you can only write about things your character has seen or heard. If you include things he or she couldn't know, it makes the story less believable.

What next?

Imagine you find a dusty old notebook. You flip through the pages and find that someone has started to write a story in it. But then, the story stops... It's up to you to finish it.

Questions to ask yourself before you start

- Who is Billy?
- How old is he?
- Why is Billy on the ship?
- What kind of ship is it – a navy vessel, a pleasure cruiser, a pirate ship?
- Who else is on board?
- Where is the ship going? Is it going to get there?
- What has Billy just seen?
- What danger lies ahead?
- How does Billy try to overcome the danger?
- Does anyone help him?
- Does anyone or anything get in his way?
- Do they find land?
- Will Billy make it home? Does he want to?

....
(Write your story title here.)

Billy clung onto the rail of the ship as the vessel tipped this way and that. It was the worst storm he'd ever seen. With one powerful lurch, he felt himself being thrown across the deck. Winded and terrified, he looked up as a flash of lightning lit up the ocean. He gasped. Just ahead of the ship's bow, he saw...

fearsome

thunder

looming

darkness

rigging

hurricane

Speaking parts

Including dialogue (speaking parts) will help bring your readers right into the action.

This is usually shown in quotation marks like this: "Quick, run!" cried Sam. "He's catching up with us," panted Nathan.

cliffs

ghostly

lightning

island

overboard

rescue

tumbling

racing

stowaway

ship's cat

hostage

treasure

tidal wave

suspense

surprise

sea monster

daydream

escape

running away

survivor

danger

captain

trouble

all of a sudden

Every picture tells a story

Write a story about the picture on the right. You could write about the whole scene, or just one part that catches your attention. You could even choose to write about something that's just out of sight.

Questions to think about

- Where is this room?
- Is it in a huge mansion or a tiny bungalow? In the countryside or at the edge of a big city? Inside a virtual reality game?
- Who's the old lady? (If that's what she really is...)
- Who is the man outside the window and what is he doing?
- What's beyond the mountains in the distance?
- Why is the eagle there?
- What are the mice up to?
- Where does the archway behind the bookshelves lead?
- Who's the woman in the painting?
- Who does the crystal ball on the table belong to?

Create your own fairy tale

....

(Write your story title here.)

Once upon a time... that's how all fairy tales begin. But now you can decide how the story goes, using the lists on these pages to help you.

Once upon a time...

Possible characters

- prince
- princess
- fairy godmother
- mermaid
- ogre
- wicked queen
- big, bad wolf

Settings

- magical castle
- underground caverns
- up a beanstalk
- house made of sweets
- bottomless well
- mysterious forest
- undersea kingdom

Objects

- flying carpet
- magic ring
- glass shoe
- enchanted mirror
- crystal ball
- spinning wheel
- wand

Build-up ideas

The main character...

- is called on a quest
- wishes for a friend
- finds something magical
- receives an invitation
- has an unexpected guest
- arrives in a strange land
- dreams of riches

Problems

This character...

- is taken prisoner
- falls under a spell
- gets lost
- is turned into a frog
- is injured
- meets an enemy
- is mistaken for someone else

Fairy tale endings

- wedding
- enemies make friends
- family reunion
- killing the dragon
- returning home
- a mystery is solved
- finding fame and fortune

doom!   monstrous

fire-breathing   sparkling

fairy wish

servant

glittering

magical

golden

terrifying   puff of smoke

merry   abracadabra!

cursed

enchanted

beautiful

FEE FI FO FUM!

handsome

cackling

happily ever after

fluttering

crown

Comic strip

Here's an unfinished comic strip about two young pirates going on an exciting treasure hunt.

The pictures have been drawn, but what are the characters saying?

Now it's up to you to tell the story by writing dialogue in the speech bubbles.

Continued...

The End.

Time travel

Imagine it's possible to travel through time. Choose a time and a place that excites you and write a story about a journey to that time.

Questions to consider

- Who travels through time and how? By accident? Or using some sort of time machine? If so, what happens if it breaks down?

- Where do your characters travel to and when?

- Do they plan to solve a mystery, to bring back future technology or to try to change the course of history?

- What problems and dangers do they come across?

- If your story is set in the past, do the characters meet any historical figures?

- How do people live, dress and get around in the time you're writing about?

- Do your characters travel back to their own time in the end?

Here are a few times and places you could write about:

- Dinosaur times

- The Stone Age

- Ancient Egypt

- The Middle Ages

- The 19th century

- The future

Period details

Historical or futuristic details about how people live — such as what their homes look like, how they communicate or what they eat — will help make your story vivid.

But don't spend too long describing the setting — what happens to the characters is much more important.

1976

2268

Family fortunes

Imagine your family suddenly inherits lots of money from a long-lost uncle, and you become instant millionaires.

But there's a catch – you also inherit something else. Something that turns your lives upside down. (It's up to you to decide what that is.)

Questions to ask yourself

- What's the first thing you buy with your new-found fortune?
- Does your family fight about how to divide the money?

- What do you inherit?

A baby?

A grumpy granny?

A dangerous animal?

A letter containing a family secret?

A creepy old house?

bickering
joking
sofa
feud
rivalry
half-sister

stepfather
show off
nagging
revelation
secret
suspicion
millionaires
luxury cruise
shock
hidden past

Superpowers

Write a story about a character who has an amazing power. But make sure your character has a weakness or two and a powerful enemy to defeat. If everything's too easy, the story could get boring.

Possible powers

- the ability to fly
- invisibility
- the ability to control the weather
- invulnerability (can't be hurt)
- telepathy (can read minds)
- telekinesis (can move objects without touching them)

Questions

- Where is the story set?
- How does your character get her or his powers?
- Are there any downsides to having them?
- What does she or he use them for? Fighting crime? Getting rich? Or something else?

- Does your character's enemy have powers too?
- What is your character's main goal? Does she or he achieve it?

The final showdown

When you're bringing your story to a close, try to include a final confrontation between your character and her or his main enemy. You could set this somewhere dramatic, such as the villain's lair.

Animal adventure

Write about a group of animals who live in a forest. One day they learn that humans are going to clear the trees and build a shopping mall. Their homes will be destroyed. What happens next?

Questions

- What kind of animals are they? Are they a family of the same species, or sworn enemies who are forced to work together?

- What is their home like? Does it have tall trees to climb or thick undergrowth to hide in? Is it hot and wet or cold and dry?

- Do the animals rely on their senses? Can they sniff out danger? Can they see or hear things that humans can't?

- What do the animals look like? Do they have thick, padded paws, slimy scales or dagger-sharp teeth?

- How do they move? Do they hop, slither or scurry?

- Do the animals defeat the humans, or do they have to find a new home?

Animal facts

Sometimes an interesting fact can lead to a great story idea, so you may find it useful to do some research into the animals you choose to write about.

silky-soft fur

scuttle

danger

frozen with fear

growl

undergrowth

whimper

snarl

bounding

burrows

crawl

slimy skin

panic

powerful

fierce

protective

rough tongue

keen-eyed

Whodunnit?

A billionaire has been found murdered in a mansion.
The murder weapon: poison.

But who is the culprit?
A detective is called to the crime scene to investigate.

Write a story describing how the mystery is solved.

When you start writing, *you* should know who did it, but don't give it away too soon.

Questions

- Is the detective a police officer or an amateur sleuth?
- How does the detective work? Slowly and scientifically? Alone or with a sidekick? By tricking the criminal into confessing?
- Who is the murderer?
- Why did he or she do it?
- Does he or she try to put the blame on someone else?
- What clues does the detective find?
- Is the murderer caught in the end? If so, how?

58

Motive:

The reason someone commits a crime.

For example, it could be revenge, for money, or out of jealousy, hatred or love.

Suspect:

Anyone who has both a motive and an opportunity to commit the crime.

Keep your readers guessing by including a few suspects with different motives.

Evidence:

The information and clues a detective finds to prove who's guilty.

These could include fingerprints, a piece of clothing, a lipstick print on a glass or the murder weapon.

Alibi:

Proof that a suspect was somewhere else at the time of the murder.

not cross CRIME SCENE Do not cross CRIME SCENE

CRIME SCENE Do not cross CRIME SCENE

police station

stake out

greed

billionaire's will

suspicious

private investigator

DNA

alibi

forensic team

magnifying glass

questioning

muddy footprints

inspector

car chase

CRIME SCENE Do not cross CRIME SCENE Do not cross

microscope

Stage school

You've just won a place at the world's most famous stage school. On your first day, you find out that all the new pupils will be performing in a show at the end of the week. Can you put together a great performance in time?

Questions

- Who's the first person you meet?
- Which class do you like best - ballet, acting, tap, modern dance, singing?
- What are the teachers like?
- What show do you do?
- What's your role in it – Actor? Dancer? Singer? Director? Set designer?
- Does anyone argue?
- What costumes do you wear?
- Where are you performing and who's watching?
- Does anything come between you and your dream? A rival student? A missing costume? An accident? Stage fright?
- Does the audience cheer at the end, or are you booed off the stage?

main part

understudy

leotard

spotlight

exercises

starstruck

stage

stretches

cafeteria

home time

piano

costume

rehearsal

disaster

curtains

The big game

There's one minute to go before the end of a big game, and it's a tie. Can anyone win the day?

Now describe the nail-biting action that follows.

Questions

- What sport is it?
- What kind of game is it? Is it the cup final in a new stadium, or a friendly game in a park?
- Do the two sides have a history of bitter rivalry?
- Are you telling the story from the point of view of a player, a manager, or a fan cheering from the sidelines?
- What's the weather like — dazzling sunshine or freezing rain?
- What if nobody scores?
- Does anyone try to break the rules?
- Do the fans agree with all the referee's decisions?
- Is there a last-minute substitution?
- Who wins the game and how do they do it?

SCORE!

substitute

attack

challenge

chase

dodge

kick dive

pass save

overtake

intercept

score

action replay

championship

strike

CHEAT!

REFEREE!

Top secret spies

Imagine that you turn on your computer, and this email message pops up:

 Subject: Help!

 Priority: URGENT

Have been captured by enemy agents. Go to location X and recover the files immediately. Then come and rescue me. Am being taken to Dead Drop C. Beware: Yellowbelly is a double-agent.

Hurry
Starfish

Now tell the story of what happens next.

Questions

- Where are location X and Dead Drop C?
- What is in the files?
- Do you have a code name?
- Who are you working for or against?
- Who are Starfish and Yellowbelly?
- How does the mission end?

Global intrigue

Spies often travel all around the world. That gives you a lot of choice of exciting settings. For example, you could take your characters to an ancient town in North Africa, an elegant café in Paris, a secret, underground bunker or up to the top of the Empire State Building.

secret organization

infiltrate

double agent

unmask

computer files

martial arts

prototype

secret weapon

undercover

follow orders

countdown

self-destruct

narrow escape

scuba diving

code word

helicopter

anonymous tip-off

intelligence

secret mission

disguise

safe house

Pony trouble

It's summertime and you're working at a local stables.

One day, your boss allows you to go out for a ride on the pony you like the best.

You stop for a picnic and tie the pony to a tree. But, unfortunately, the pony comes untied and runs away. Gulp!

Write a story about what happens next.

Questions

- Where does the pony go? Are you in remote countryside or on the edge of a town?
- Who owns the pony? What will happen if you don't get it back?
- What dangers might you or the pony come across? Are you near a busy road, a dense forest, or a fast-flowing river?
- Does anyone help you find the pony along the way?
- Does anyone try to get in your way?
- Do you get the pony back safely?
- How does your boss react (if you own up, that is)?

riding hat

canter

whinnying

whip

gallop

mucking out

stallion

woodland

winding lane

saddle

horseshoe

escape

bridle

fast cars

sweaty

hoof prints

muddy

Your story: the movie

CAST LIST

Imagine that a Hollywood executive in a very expensive suit knocks on your door. She smiles at you with her perfect teeth and says she has news for you.

One of your stories is being made into a movie. (Pause to scream! Gasp! Call everyone you have ever met!)

But there are still important decisions to be made: who should play the characters in your story on the big screen?

Choose one of your stories and come up with a cast to play all the characters in it. You could cast famous actors, or your friends and family.

Pick some songs for the soundtrack too.

You could use this page to make a note of any interesting words that you come across.

Story Writing Toolkit

This section has lots of tips to help you plan your stories and develop your writing skills. There's also space for you to write lists of words that spark your imagination, and to jot down ideas for more stories.

Giving your stories great titles

Sometimes, you might come up with a fantastic story title before you've even written the story. Other times you might wait to see how a story turns out before you decide what to call it. Whenever you pick your title, make sure it's something that will make other people really curious to read it.

Story titles can be effective because they are funny like *The runaway pancake*, mysterious like *The dark, dark knight*, intriguing like *How the elephant lost its wings* or exciting like *Kidnapped*. Think of some stories you've read or heard about that have titles you like. List them here so you can look back at them when you're thinking up your own titles.

Think up as many different titles as you can.

Now try writing titles for these story ideas.

Story ideas:	Possible titles:
The adventures of a talking dog.	
A boy who has a dinosaur for a pet.	
A princess who dreams of becoming an astronaut.	

In the beginning...

The beginning of your story is where you introduce your main character and something happens to get the story started. When you're writing the beginning of your story, include something that will grab the reader's attention.

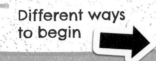

Different ways to begin

- Start with a person talking, so your reader immediately "meets" one of your characters by hearing his or her voice:

"You can't expect me to go out looking like this!" exclaimed the Queen.

- Begin with some action:

Dean stepped on the gas, but the other driver was gaining on him.

- Open your story by describing its setting:

It was midnight, and moonlight slanted through the trees onto the forest floor.

Choose one of your story titles and try out some different opening lines here.

Plant seeds for later

Think about including something near the beginning of your story that will be important later. For example, this could be a clue that will help to solve a mystery. Or it could be a mention of the villain's weakness that will allow the hero to beat him or her in the end.

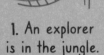

Story rollercoaster

The middle of your story is where most of the action takes place.
To keep your readers gripped, it's a good idea to give your character a tricky problem
to overcome. If one problem leads to another, the story will feel more exciting.
So you could think of it as a rollercoaster ride with several ups and downs.

Here's an example of a rollercoaster for an adventure story:

2. He heads off on a trek.

4. He finds a wooden bridge.

6. He lands safely in the water.

1. An explorer is in the jungle.

3. He needs to cross a deep, wide river.

5. But the bridge breaks under his weight.

7. But the water's full of crocodiles.

Here's a story starter with blanks for you to fill in your own story rollercoaster. The problems could be dramatic and scary, or they could be simple and realistic, depending on the kind of story you prefer. For example, a problem could be your character saying something embarrassing, and the solution could be another character telling a joke to distract everyone.

2. Inside, he finds a winning lottery ticket.

4.

6.

1. A boy receives an envelope with his name on it.

3.

5.

7.

Remember your story can't just keep going, and then…
and then… and then. Eventually you need to reach an ending…

Happily ever after?

Bringing a story to a close isn't simply a matter of writing "The End" when you run out of ideas. The ending should feel satisfying, like the last bite of a delicious meal. It's where the story's problems are solved and the loose threads of the story are tied up – although that doesn't necessarily mean the characters all end up problem-free and happy.

Here are a few suggestions for different story endings. Can you think of some more? (There are some questions for you to ask yourself on the right.)

- At last, they were home.

- The spaceship hurtled to safety as the planet exploded beneath them.

- ...and they lived happily ever after.

- From then on, he never did anything that dangerous again.

- Everyone agreed that it had been a very unusual day.

- Luke gasped in amazement. "So it was you all along!" he cried.

How does it end?

- Does the story end happily or sadly, or is it more complicated than that?
- Is there a twist or a surprise at the end?
- Does the main character finally overcome his or her problems and difficulties?
- Is there a hero who defeats a villain in the end?
- Is a mystery solved?
- Is a lesson learned at the end?
- Is everything resolved or are there any questions left unanswered?

Learning from other writers

When you're thinking of endings for your own stories, you could use your experience as a reader to help you as a writer. Make a note of endings you have read and liked. Were they happy, sad, surprising or clever? How did they make you feel?

Heroes and villains

Whether you're writing about heroes, villains, unusual creatures or ordinary people, if you come up with strong, interesting characters they can often lead to some exciting story ideas.

Here are a few character ideas. Can you add some more that you'll want to write stories about later?

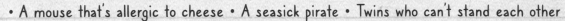

- A mouse that's allergic to cheese • A seasick pirate • Twins who can't stand each other
- A maid who rebels against the queen • A boy who invents lots of crazy gadgets
- A fairy whose spells keep going wrong • A girl who builds a home in a tree

Picture perfect
Sometimes, drawing pictures of your characters can help you decide what they're like.

Location, location

When you're creating a world for your story, you can really bring it to life for your readers if you describe what the place looks, sounds, feels and even smells like. You can also use the setting to help set the mood of your story. For example, you could set a happy story at a beach party, or a scary one in a gloomy forest.

Here are a few possible settings with space for you to add lots more to use later.

- Undersea city • Dragon's den • Hockey tournament • Dinosaur zoo
- Desert island • Animal rescue clinic • Medieval castle • Fairyland • Wild West

Be observant

Wherever you go, make a note of the sights and sounds that interest you about that place. You never know when you might stumble upon the setting for your next story.

Exciting writing

When it comes to writing, it's not enough to have a gripping plot, believable characters or an atmospheric setting — the words you use to describe them make a big difference to how enjoyable your story is to read. So try to think of interesting adjectives (describing words) and verbs (doing words).

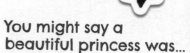

Adjectives

Common adjectives include big, small, ugly, beautiful, bad and good. But there are so many others to choose from, make sure you don't always use the same ones.

A small animal could be...
- little
- puny
- tiny
- dinky
-
-
-
-

You might say a beautiful princess was...
- dazzling
- pretty
- ravishing
- stunning
-
-
-

An exciting adventure might be...
- action-packed
- intrepid
- perilous
- thrilling
-
-
-
-

An Egyptian tomb could be described as...
- ancient
- dusty
- eerie
- towering
-
-
-
-

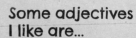

Some adjectives I like are...
-
-
-
-
-
-
-
-

My love is like a red, red rose...

To give a clearer picture of the thing you're describing, you could compare it to something else. So you might say, "a monster is as tall as a skyscraper," or "a fairy's voice tinkles like a bell." This kind of comparison is known as a simile. Try writing some of your own here.

Verbs

These tell you what a character or thing does, thinks or feels and can reflect a person's mood or personality.

When I'm in a hurry, I...
- rush
- panic
- speed
- sprint
-
-
-
-

When I'm with my friends, I...
- laugh
- joke
- play
- chatter
-
-
-
-

When I'm angry, I...
- shout
- sulk
- stamp
- scowl
-
-
-
-
-

Beware of the adverb!

Adverbs are words which describe verbs – for example, quickly, loudly or suddenly.

But adverbs can make your writing sound clumsy. If you use more interesting verbs, you can avoid using adverbs altogether, and say what you mean more concisely. For example, instead of, "She stood up quickly from her seat and shouted loudly," you could say, "She sprang from her seat and bellowed."

Telling tales

If you want to add richer detail and greater depth to your writing, you could try using different styles and points of view to see which suits your stories best.

Experiment with your sentences...

You can tell the same story many different ways.
For example, you could write:

The boy ran along the street. He was being chased by a tiger.

but you could also write:

Panting for breath, the boy raced along the street. The tiger was getting close!

or you could put it like this:

"Help!" cried Tommy. His short legs were pumping as fast as they could go. "There's a tiger after me! Help!"

Adding speech, like this, helps to bring drama to your stories, and makes your characters more convincing.

All in the past?

Whether you choose to write in the past or present tense can make a big difference to the impact of your story. Most stories are written in the past tense, because it's usually what comes most naturally:

Once, upon a time, there were three bears.

But the present tense can be useful, especially if you want to draw your readers into the action — as though it's taking place right in front of them:

So I'm walking down the road, minding my own business when all of a sudden...

Take care! Your story will become confusing if you switch from one tense to another. It's best to choose one and stick to it.

Points of view

The "voice" you use to tell a story is known as the narrator. You can achieve different effects depending on the point of view you choose for your narrator.

"I/We" point of view = First person:

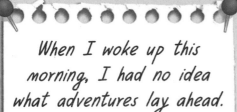

When I woke up this morning, I had no idea what adventures lay ahead.

This point of view helps to make a story seem personal, as though it's being told by someone involved in the events. But, it can be limited. The narrator may not know the whole story, and can only talk about what he or she knows.

"You" point of view = Second person:

You know you're in trouble when the boss gives you one of his looks.

This is an unusual point of view, but it can be an effective way of bringing the reader closer to the narrator, as though they are both in it together.

"He/She/They" point of view = Third person:

A burly figure strode across the deck, his crimson frockcoat flapping in the sea breeze. Where his left hand should have been, a silver hook gleamed.

Here, the narrator describes a scene almost as though he or she is watching a movie. This is the point of view writers use most often. It allows you to get inside the mind of more than one character and gives your readers a chance to see the story from different angles.

Short, short stories

If you want to give your imagination a workout, you could try writing micro-stories. These should have a beginning, a middle and an end, just as longer stories do. The only difference is that they should be short enough to fit on a single piece of paper or in a text message. There's no room to waffle, so make sure every word counts.

Try writing a micro-version of a story you've read and loved. How far can you boil it down without losing the best parts?

Use a snippet of conversation you have overheard as the starting point for a micro-story. It could be something you've heard at home, in the street or on a bus.

Imagine going on the journey of a lifetime. How would you travel? Who would you take with you? Where would you go and what would you do when you got there?

Use a saying or proverb, such as "pigs might fly", as the inspiration for a story.

Think of an intriguing old object you've seen in a shop window or in a museum. Imagine where it might have come from and who once owned it. Does its past hold any secrets?

Keep on writing

It's a myth that all great writers were born that way. Writing stories, like any skill, is something you get better at the more you do it.

Here are some tips to help you polish your skills.

Ask people to read your stories and tell you what they think of them – good AND bad.

Keep a diary. Write in it when you feel happy. Write in it when you feel sad. Write in it when you're not sure how you feel. Write down your secrets (and hide them, obviously). Write down all the funny things you hear.

Go for walks and tell yourself stories about what you see.

Write a blog about something you're passionate about.

Write a sequel to a story you've enjoyed reading. What happens next to the characters?

Write sequels to your own stories, or turn them into plays.

Keep a notebook with you wherever you go so you can write whenever an idea comes to you. If you have a spare moment, take out your notebook and write the first thing that comes into your head.

Whenever you see a word you don't understand, look it up in a dictionary and then use it in your writing.

Draw pictures of your thoughts.

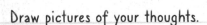

Write for your school magazine or newspaper. If you don't have one, maybe you could start one?

Talk to people you've never talked to before at school.

Write long emails to your friends and family.

Ask friends and relatives to tell you about their lives. Can you find beginnings of new stories in there somewhere?

Read a lot and write book reviews.

Acknowledgements

This is the part of your book where you thank anyone who's helped you while you were writing it. Parents? Friends? Teachers? Loyal fans? Famous authors who have inspired you? Thank them here:

- ---------------------------------------
- ---------------------------------------
- ---------------------------------------

These people helped out too:

The people who set you challenges and gave you tips:

Louie Stowell

Megan Cullis · · · · · · · · · · · · Alex Frith

Susanna Davidson · · · · · · · Rob Lloyd Jones

Kate Davies · · · · · · · · · · · · Lesley Sims

The person who drew all the pictures:
Katie Lovell

The person who designed it all:
Suzie Harrison

The people who made sure everything made sense:
Ruth Brocklehurst · · · Jane Chisholm · · · Jenny Tyler

This edition first published in 2023 by Usborne Publishing Limited, 83-85 Saffron Hill, London ECIN 8RT, United Kingdom. usborne.com